# The Ktunaxa

**ERINN BANTING**

**Weigl**

CALGARY
www.weigl.com

Published by Weigl Educational Publishers Limited
6325 10 Street SE
Calgary, Alberta, Canada
T2H 2Z9

Website: www.weigl.com

Library and Archives Canada Cataloguing in Publication data available upon request.
Fax (403) 233-7769 for the attention of the Publishing Records department.

ISBN 978-1-55388-428-6 (hard cover)
ISBN 978-1-55388-429-3 (soft cover)

Printed in the United States of America
1 2 3 4 5 6 7 8 9 0  12 11 10 09 08

**Project Coordinator** Heather Kissock   **Design** Janine Vangool   **Layout** Kathryn Livingstone
**Validator** Janice and Dorothy Alpine

**Photograph credits**
Every reasonable effort has been made to trace ownership and to obtain permission to reprint copyright
material. The publishers would be pleased to have any errors or omissions brought to their attention so that
they may be corrected in subsequent printings.

**Cover (main):** With permission of the Royal Ontario Museum © ROM; **Cover (top left):** Gerry Ward, Canmore
Museum and Geoscience Centre: **Cover (top centre):** Alamy; **Cover (top right):** Getty Images; **Alamy:** page 5, 16,
18; **All Canada Photos:** page 19; **Canadian Museum of Civilization:** pages 3 (1977-104-617, D2005-16065), 14 (II-A-
105, D2002-007955), 24 (1977-104-617, D2005-16065), 28 (II-A-156, D2002-007952); **Corbis:** page 13; **Doreen Manuel:**
page 27; **Gerry Ward, Canmore Museum and Geoscience Centre:** page 26; **Getty Images:** pages 12, 17, 21, 23;
**Royal British Columbia Museum:** pages 6, 7, 10, 11, 14, 15, 20, 25; **With permission of the Royal Ontario Museum
© ROM:** pages 10, 11.

We acknowledge the financial support of the Government of Canada through the Book Publishing Industry
Development Program (BPIDP) for our publishing activities.

**Please note**
All of the Internet URLs given in the book were valid at the time of publication. However, due to the dynamic
nature of the Internet, some addresses may have changed, or sites may have ceased to exist since publication.
While the author and publisher regret any inconvenience this may cause readers, no responsibility for any such
changes can be accepted by either the author or the publisher.

# CONTENTS

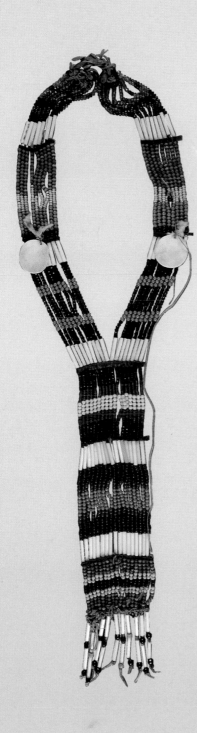

# The People

The Ktunaxa (pronounced 'k-too-nah-ha') are a **First Nations** group that lives in southeastern British Columbia, Canada, as well as Montana and Idaho, in the United States. In the past, their territory extended through the Rocky Mountain and **Interior Plains** regions of North America and included settlements in Alberta and the state of Washington.

The Ktunaxa were divided into two groups. These groups were based on which side of the Kootenay River they lived. The Upper Ktunaxa lived on the eastern side of the river in parts of British Columbia, Alberta, and Montana. The Lower Ktunaxa lived on the western side of the river in parts of British Columbia, Idaho, and Washington.

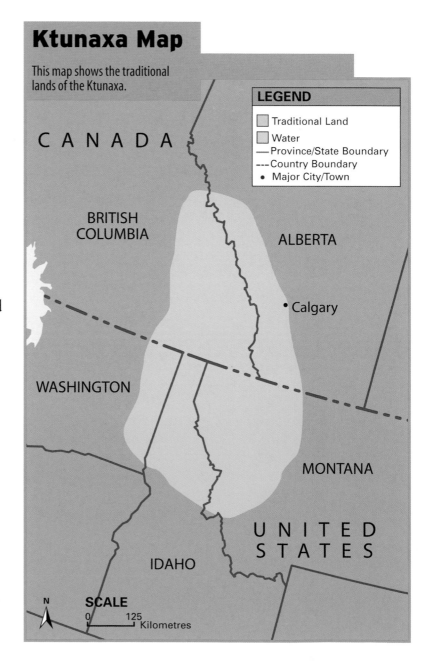

## Ktunaxa Map

This map shows the traditional lands of the Ktunaxa.

LEGEND
- Traditional Land
- Water
- Province/State Boundary
- Country Boundary
- Major City/Town

CANADA

BRITISH COLUMBIA

ALBERTA

• Calgary

WASHINGTON

MONTANA

UNITED STATES

IDAHO

N

SCALE
0    125
Kilometres

The Ktunaxa are known by many different names, including the Kootenay, Kootenai, or Kootenae. There are different theories about the origin of the Ktunaxa name. One theory proposes that the origin of the name is from the Ktunaxa word *Quthni*, which means "to travel by water." Another theory suggests that the name comes from the Blackfoot word *Kutunåiua*, meaning "slim people." The traditional lands of the Blackfoot neighbour those of the Ktunaxa.

Beginning in the 1500s, the booming **fur trade** brought European explorers to what is now Canada in search of new trade routes and plentiful goods. The Ktunaxa became very important to the expansion of the fur trade in Alberta and British Columbia in the 1700s and 1800s.

Today, many Ktunaxa live on **reserve lands** in British Columbia, Idaho, and Montana. Some also live in towns and cities across Canada and the United States. Many Ktunaxa work hard to combine modern conveniences with their traditions and history.

One of the most interesting examples of this dedication to building on history is the recently constructed Ktunaxa Kinbasket Interpretive Centre, near Cranbrook, British Columbia. The centre is an interactive museum that includes **artifacts**, multimedia displays, and other exhibits. It is housed in what was once an **Aboriginal residential school**. A golf course and hotel complex have also been built on the site.

Many natural landmarks and parks were named after the Ktunaxa, including Kootenay National Park.

# Ktunaxa Homes

Traditionally, the spring and summer months were busy times for the Ktunaxa. They moved often as they followed herds of **migrating** animals, such as bison. As a result of this constant movement, they needed homes that were portable, or could be put up and taken down easily.

The Upper Ktunaxa built teepees made from long poles tied together in a cone shape. The poles were covered in animal skins. This helped keep the Ktunaxa warm in the high, mountainous regions in which they lived.

The Lower Ktunaxa also built teepees. They covered their poles with reeds instead of animal skins. This is because the weather was warmer in their region. The reeds let cool breezes pass through.

Unlike other First Nations groups, the Ktunaxa did not paint designs on their teepees. They were kept plain.

Both the Upper and Lower Ktunaxa built permanent shelters. These were used in winter when the Ktunaxa did not migrate. They were often built near the banks of rivers and lakes.

Ktunaxa winter homes were long, lodge-like structures. Some had floors that were partially sunken into the ground. Others were built completely aboveground. Reed mats covered the outside of the building. The mats protected the people living in the house from the cold.

Ktunaxa encampments could be found throughout Ktunaxa traditional lands.

# Ktunaxa Communities

Family and community have always been very important to the Ktunaxa. In the past, their survival depended on cooperation within families and communities. People had to work together in order to survive.

Whole communities lived and travelled together from camp to camp during migration seasons. They worked together to pack up their possessions and move from one location to another. Once the site of a camp was chosen, the men of the community set up the teepees. They then were responsible for hunting or fishing, while the women gathered nuts and berries, cared for the children, made clothing, and prepared food for the group.

Huckleberries were one kind of berry Ktunaxa women picked. They normally ripen in mid to late summer.

Ktunaxa communities were led by several chiefs, who were each responsible for particular tasks at certain times. Some chiefs made decisions regarding where to set up camps. Others decided where to hunt. Chiefs consulted with **elders** and other leaders to make decisions that protected and helped the entire community. They were assisted in these tasks by special societies, made up of people who performed certain functions within the community, such as policing and healing.

Today, many Ktunaxa live in permanent settlements on reserve lands. They have incorporated modern conveniences and advances in communication, technology, and transportation into their day-to-day lives. They have combined these advances with the traditions of their elders to preserve their unique **culture** and communities.

Today, Ktunaxa communities are still led by chiefs. The communities follow their own form of government and elect their leaders the same way leaders are elected throughout Canada.

Ktunaxa communities in Canada and the United States work together through the Ktunaxa Nation Council. Leaders and members of the communities gather and communicate regularly to address issues affecting the Ktunaxa. They work to protect their land rights, their culture, and the education of their people.

**Ktunaxa families were large, consisting of grandparents, parents, and children living together as a single unit.**

# Ktunaxa Clothing

Traditional Ktunaxa clothing was made from materials found in nature. The Ktunaxa relied on furs and hides from the animals they hunted to make durable, warm, and waterproof clothing. Women wore long dresses made from animal hides. In colder weather, they also wore leggings. Men wore shirts and leggings made from animal hides. In winter, warm coats made from fur helped keep them warm.

Ktunaxa jewellery was made of items found in nature, such as stones and animal teeth.

Both women and men wore **moccasins** to keep their feet warm and protected. There were two types of moccasins. Low-top moccasins covered only the feet and ankles. High-top moccasins looked more like boots and covered the feet and part of the calf. They were laced up with strips of leather tied around the calf.

The Ktunaxa decorated their hair with accessories made from leather and feathers. During battle or celebrations, men wore elaborate headdresses made from feathers. They also wore hair roaches. Hair roaches were made up of a round piece of leather with porcupine quills attached to it. The roaches were fastened around the wearer's head with a leather strap.

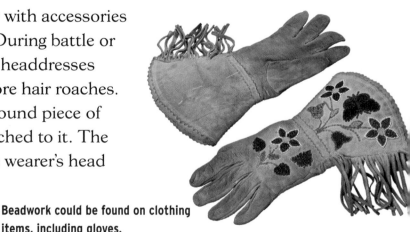

Beadwork could be found on clothing items, including gloves.

**Baby carriers were also given elaborate beadwork designs.**

When European traders arrived in the area, they introduced fabric and coloured glass beads to the Ktunaxa. These materials were incorporated into traditional Ktunaxa clothing. Many Ktunaxa adopted the European style of dress. They used the fabrics to make shirts, blouses, dresses, and pants.

Today, the Ktunaxa celebrate their **ancestors** and **heritage** by wearing traditional clothing at special events and celebrations. Elders in Ktunaxa communities have passed down the art of making clothing from generation to generation. Artisans make the clothing as a way of recognizing their heritage. Many communities also sell clothing, such as moccasins, outside their communities.

In the past, the Ktunaxa had clothing for everyday use, as well as clothing they wore for special occasions. Dance **regalia**, for example, had features that everyday clothing did not. Women's dancing dresses featured colourful materials and many layers so that the women would look like floating butterflies when they danced. Men's regalia featured fringes that looked like grasses or reeds blowing in the wind.

**Besides beads, Ktunaxa clothing could be decorated with horsehair and paint.**

# Ktunaxa Food

The Ktunaxa used the natural resources and animals they hunted to provide them with shelter and food. Beginning in the early spring, the Ktunaxa would follow migrating herds of bison, deer, caribou, and elk. In the mountains, the Ktunaxa also hunted goats and bighorn sheep. Groups that lived closer to water also fished and hunted wild birds, such as geese.

The Ktunaxa also relied on the many plants the grew in the area. Saskatoon berries and chokecherries were used to make **pemmican** and jams, both of which could be stored and eaten over the winter months. Bitterroot was dug up in the spring and used in stews, soups, and gravies. When dried, bitterroot also could last over the winter.

**Bighorn sheep are common in the mountainous Kootenay area of British Columbia.**

## Bitterroot Pudding

Ingredients

0.5 litre Saskatoon berries (canned)

60 millilitres cup bitterroot

30 mL flour

Equipment

**saucepan**

**wooden spoon**

**stove**

Directions

1. Place bitterroot in saucepan.

2. Add canned Saskatoon berries.

3. Stir and bring both to a soft boil.

4. Add flour, and continue to stir until mixture thickens.

5. Eat the pudding right away or store it in refrigerator until needed.

# Tools and Weapons

The traditional tools and weapons used by the Ktunaxa were made from materials in their natural surroundings. Wood, stone, and animal bones were used to make items needed for everyday use.

The Ktunaxa believed that all the parts of an animal should be used after it was killed. Animal bones were strong and durable, and were used to make many of the items needed at camp. They were carved to make utensils, including spoons, and sharpened to make tools, such as hide scrapers. Hide scrapers were used to clean the skins of animals so they could be made into blankets or clothing. The hides were also used to make bags and water bottles.

Men used items from nature to make weapons and hunting tools as well. Knives, spears, and arrowheads were made by sharpening stone, and sometimes bone. The bone or stone was then fastened to tree branches with twine or animal hide.

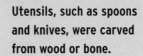

Utensils, such as spoons and knives, were carved from wood or bone.

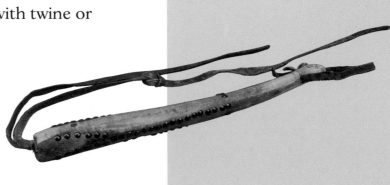

Quirts were whip-like tools used to move animals.

# TRANSPORTATION

Travelling by water was an important part of Ktunaxa life. Canoes were their main form of transportation on the area's many lakes and rivers. The Ktunaxa are well known for the design of their canoes. **Sturgeon**-nose canoes had pointed tips at the bottom. This helped to cut through fast-moving currents and kept water from spilling into the canoes.

Up to six different types of tree could be used to make a sturgeon-nose canoe. Pine bark normally formed the underside of the canoe, while birchbark formed the **gunwale**. These pieces were sewn together with cedar roots. Willow was often used to create the ribs that formed the frame. Some canoes also included Douglas fir, maple, and bitter cherry trees in their construction.

To begin building the canoe, a pattern was marked on the ground using stakes. The ribs and gunwales were then attached to the stakes. The bark was sewn to the ribs, with an additional layer of bark placed on top of that layer. At either end of the canoe, several layers of bark were folded over willow rings. These layers were then shaped into a point and sewn, giving the canoe its unique sturgeon-nose appearance.

The land the Ktunaxa inhabited had many waterways, making the canoe a necessity.

# Ktunaxa Religion

The Ktunaxa believe it is important to cooperate with and respect the land, as well as their family, community, and ancestors. Many Ktunaxa beliefs centre on paying respect to the people, animals, and natural landmarks in their communities.

The Ktunaxa have a strong spiritual connection with the Kootenay River.

These traditional beliefs have existed for thousands of years. When Europeans settled western Canada, however, they brought their **Christian** beliefs and introduced them to the Ktunaxa. Many Ktunaxa became Christian as a result. Their traditional beliefs were in danger of being lost.

In recent years, the Ktunaxa have started programs to protect their traditional beliefs and practices, and pass them on to younger generations. Today, most Ktunaxa have returned to their traditional **spirituality**.

A creation story tells how people came to live on Earth. The Ktunaxa creation story describes a sea monster that created many problems for the land animals. The land animals decided to capture the monster and destroy it. Once this was achieved, people were made from different parts of the monster.

In the 1800s, Europeans came to the Ktunaxa's traditional lands and began teaching their religions to the Ktunaxa.

# Ceremonies and Celebrations

The Ktunaxa hold celebrations and festivals throughout the year. Many of these celebrations give thanks to the spirits that guide and protect them. They also honour the land, animals, and communities in which the Ktunaxa live. Some celebrations mark important times in people's lives, such as a birth or a marriage.

Many Ktunaxa ceremonies are rooted in stories from long ago. The Bear Ceremonial is performed to ask the bear spirit to use its special powers to protect and guide the Ktunaxa as they hunt for food. The bear is an important figure to the Ktunaxa. A story from long ago tells of a boy who was rescued by a grizzly bear and raised as her own. The bear shows the boy how to live as a bear and how to perform the Bear Ceremonial. Through this experience, the boy gains respect for bears and receives many of their special powers. When he is older, he returns to his community, where he shares his knowledge with his people.

The Ktunaxa honour the bear as a guardian, or a spirit that watches over them.

Some Ktunaxa ceremonies show the group's spiritual connection to the land. Certain sites within their traditional land are considered **sacred** and are only used for specific purposes. Body painting played a role in many Ktunaxa ceremonies. One of the materials used to paint the body was red ochre, a type of clay. To get the ochre, the Ktunaxa had to travel to a place called the Paint Pots, in present-day Kootenay Provincial Park. The site is still considered sacred to the Ktunaxa.

The Ktunaxa in Canada and the United States work hard to preserve their traditions and teach younger generations about their celebrations and beliefs. Powwows are celebrations that combine dance, singing, storytelling, and crafts. Ktunaxa communities hold these special celebrations throughout the year.

The Paint Pots were formed by the gathering of iron oxide around cold mineral springs.

# TRADITIONAL GAME

Ktunaxa celebrations often included games for children to play. Today, the Ktunaxa continue to play the games of their ancestors.

One game is called "Turn About." To begin, a group of children hold hands and form a circle. One child stands in the middle of the circle. The children in the group begin circling the child, holding their arms in the air. As they move, they draw closer to the lone child. When they reach the child, they start moving back again, still moving in their circle.

The child then tries to hit the back of each child in the group. When someone in the group is tagged, he or she falls to the ground. The game is over when every child has been tagged.

# Music and Dance

Music and dance have always been important to the Ktunaxa. Through song and movement, the Ktunaxa tell stories, pay respect to their land and communities, and celebrate important events. Today, Ktunaxa communities still come together to watch and participate in these traditional art forms.

The Grass Dance is one of the traditional dances the Ktunaxa perform. This dance is traditionally performed by men to prepare for a powwow. The purpose of the dance is to stomp down the tall grasses to provide a surface to hold the powwow.

Drums play a key role in Ktunaxa performances and celebrations. Drummers sit in a circle and pound drums with drumsticks to create the beat for dancers to follow. The drum has great spiritual meaning to the Ktunaxa. It is always treated with respect.

Drumsticks are made from wood and animal hide.

Drums are made by stretching animal hides over wooden frames.

In the past, songs and singing were a part of everyday life for the Ktunaxa. They had songs that were sung to prepare for a hunt, when picking berries, and following a battle. Other songs were performed at celebrations, festivals, and religious ceremonies. Singers were accompanied by drumming and often danced while they sang.

Today, the Ktunaxa sing traditional songs at special events and celebrations. The songs are often sung by groups, who echo the lead singers by repeating notes and sounds. Ktunaxa songs tell stories of the past, the history of the Ktunaxa, and help pass the culture and traditions of the people down from generation to generation.

Songs often accompanied everyday tasks, such as berry picking.

# Language and Storytelling

The Ktunaxa language is one of the original Aboriginal languages of Canada. This means it is distinct from other Aboriginal languages and has its own features, pronunciations, and words that do not correspond to the languages of other Aboriginal groups. The Ktunaxa language is in grave danger of being lost because it is so different from other Aboriginal languages. The Ktunaxa have plans to keep their language alive.

Traditionally, Ktunaxa is an oral language. This means it is only used in spoken form. The Ktunaxa are now developing a written form of the language so that it may be preserved for future generations. Steps are also being taken to teach Ktunaxa children to speak their traditional language. Today, elders and educators teach children the oral language in schools and at special summer camps. Many stories are told orally, and continue to be passed down from generation to generation.

Ktunaxa is unique among the world's languages. It is not related to any other language.

| Ktunaxa | English |
| --- | --- |
| Kisuk kiyukyit | greeting and farewell |
| Patkiy | woman |
| Ká´ma | Thank you |
| Kapa'pa | grandparent (grandson speaking) |
| Ti´tkat | male child |
| Xa·xa | crow |
| Xaxas | skunk |

Ktunaxa elders use storytelling to teach their communities about the history and traditions of their people. In the past, children were told stories to teach them right from wrong. Many of these stories feature the mischievous character, Coyote. By hearing about Coyote's adventures, children learned about the pitfalls of greed and how to respect all living things.

**In Ktunaxa stories, the coyote often has unique ways of solving problems.**

One day, Coyote sees his brother Fox eating a chicken on the road. Fox agrees to let Coyote taste his chicken. Coyote loves the taste so much that he decides to find a chicken for himself. He walks for miles but cannot find a chicken. Nightfall comes, and Coyote still has not eaten.

The next morning, he decides to ask Fox where he found the chicken. Before he gets far, however, he finds a large group of chickens and quickly snatches one.

The chicken begs Coyote not to hurt her. Coyote thinks about it and decides to keep the chicken and force her to lay eggs. This way, he will never go hungry again.

That night, when Coyote goes to sleep, Chicken calls for her friends to rescue her. The other chickens are angry at Coyote for capturing their friend, so they use their beaks to pick at him until only bones remain.

The next day, Fox finds the bones of his brother and brings him back to life. He scolds Coyote for being greedy and asks if he has learned his lesson. Of course, Coyote has not.

# Ktunaxa Art

Ktunaxa artists are inspired by the history of their people, their stories, and their struggles and victories. Ktunaxa artists are also inspired by the landscapes and communities where they live. Arts and crafts, including beading and weaving, are a way to give thanks to the spirits that help and protect them.

The Ktunaxa are well known for their elaborate beadwork. Traditionally, porcupine quills were used to decorate clothing, ceremonial outfits, and even some tools and instruments. The quills were dyed to bring colour to the designs, which were often patterned using geometric shapes. Following the arrival of European settlers, glass or brass beads and floral patterns were incorporated into Ktunaxa beadwork.

**Beaded necklaces could be quite large, covering much of the chest when worn.**

Weaving is another traditional Ktunaxa art. Containers, baskets, sacks, and bags were woven from tree roots, reeds, grasses, and bark. The sinew of animals was often woven in with the plant materials, especially when making a basket. Ktunaxa baskets were made in an outward spiral shape. The sinew helped hold the spiral in place so that the basket could be used to hold the items that needed to be carried.

Special occassions, such as powwows, called for different types of clothing accessories. One type of accessory men were known to carry was the fan. Men's fans were very decorative. They were made from the feathers of large birds, such as hawks. The feathers were spread out to look like the wings of the birds in flight. Elaborate beadwork designs covered the handles of the fans. Leather strips or strips of fabric hung from the fans, adding to the beauty of their design.

**Baskets could be ornamental, with fancy designs, or more simple in structure.**

# Rock Carvings

Throughout the traditional lands of the Ktunaxa are rock carvings called petroglyphs. The Ktunaxa often created these paintings when travelling on land routes. They served as messages to people who may be following the same route. The petroglyphs were used to tell these people what is ahead as well as to provide direction.

The paintings were made using a technique called "pecking and grinding." The Ktunaxa would use stone or metal tools to scratch, or peck, patterns into the rock. They would then use a piece of wood, water, and sand to grind and smooth the edges of the scratching.

In recent years, Ktunaxa petroglyphs have become tourist attractions. Some of the people visiting the sites, however, have not been respectful of the paintings. In at least one case, the petroglyphs had to be removed from the site in order to protect them from further **vandalism**.

Most Ktunaxa petroglyphs are found around Kootenay Lake, but they can be found in other rocky areas as well.

# MODERN ARTIST

## Doreen Manuel

Doreen Manuel's artistic skills range from traditional to high-tech. She is known mainly for her work in **videography** and film, but also uses her leatherwork and beading skills to express her creativity. In all the art she creates, however, her First Nations heritage remains central.

Doreen is the sixth and youngest child of George and Marceline Manuel. Her father's side of the family is Secwepemc, while her mother's side is Ktunaxa. Doreen's father was an influential chief who made great strides in advocating the rights of Aboriginal peoples within Canada and around the world. George Manuel's work in this area had great impact on his children, including Doreen.

Much of Doreen's videography and filmwork is focussed on First Nations stories and issues. She has produced videos on AIDS in the Aboriginal community and Aboriginal foster parenting, as well as a **docudrama** about her father and a CD compilation of his speeches. Along with her filmwork, she also found the time to act as the executive producer of a play entitled *Every Warrior's Song*.

As an artist, Doreen maintains a connection with the traditional arts of her people. She was taught the skills of hide tanning, leatherwork, and beading by her maternal grandmother and her mother, and has continued to develop these skills and experiment with them in new ways. This includes applying beadwork patterns to running shoes and other clothing items.

Doreen works hard to pass her knowledge on to future generations. She is teaching her children the traditional Ktunaxa beading and leatherwork that her mother and grandmother taught her. As well, she is currently the program director of the Indigenous Independent Digital Filmmaking program at Capilano College in Vancouver, British Columbia.

**Doreen enjoys beadwork and sees similarities between beadwork and painting.**

# Studying the Past

Archaeologists use items from the past to learn about ancient cultures. Artifacts left by the Ktunaxa and their ancestors give archaeologists clues about what life was like hundreds and thousands of years ago.

Pottery, tools, and the remains of camping sites tell archaeologists much about early Ktunaxa life. They also provide information on where the Ktunaxa migrated and settled. Artifacts have been found in British Columbia, Alberta, Washington, Montana, and Idaho. They show archaeologists how the Ktunaxa used their environment to create the clothing, tools, and other objects they needed in the past.

Ktunaxa artifacts are displayed at museums throughout Canada. Stone arrowheads, canoes, fishing traps, snowshoes, baskets, and ceremonial clothing help teach people more about Ktunaxa history and traditional culture.

Ktunaxa horse saddles are just one type of artifact displayed in Canadian museums.

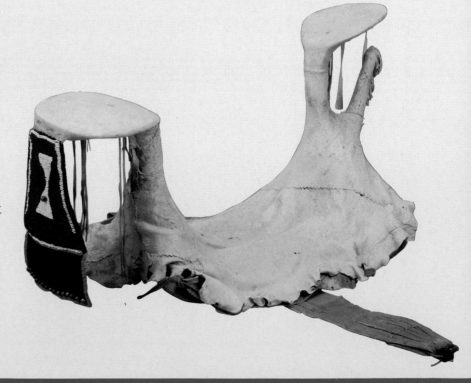

# TIMELINE

## 12,000 BC–1500 AD

Ancestors of the Ktunaxa live in western Canada and the United States. They survive by hunting caribou, elk, and buffalo. They also fish and collect berries and nuts.

## 1500–1700

The booming fur trade brings Europeans west across Canada and the United States. Settlers from England and France dispute ownership of First Nations land. Traders and explorers enlist help from First Nations people to expand their territory and the fur trade.

## 1763–1800

The fur trade reaches Ktunaxa land. The Ktunaxa meet English explorer, David Thompson, who names them the "Kootenay." The Ktunaxa are introduced to European tools and goods.

## 1830–1870

Gold is discovered in the West, and thousands of people move to British Columbia and the Ktunaxa lands.

## 1876–1960

Canada's Indian Act is put into effect. As a result of this act, the Ktunaxa are moved onto reserves, and their children are placed in residential schools.

## 1960–1970

Residential schools are phased out. Children are returned to their families, placed in foster homes, or adopted into non-Aboriginal families.

## 1970–1980

The Kootenay Indian District Council is formed to promote Ktunaxa culture and independence.

## 1990

The Kootenay Indian District Council changes its name to the Ktunaxa/Kinbasket Tribal Council.

## 2005

The Ktunaxa Nation Council is formed. The group works to protect Ktunaxa traditions and history.

**Elk still roam the Ktunaxa's traditional lands.**

# Make a Lane Stitch Choker

Powwow regalia normally features vibrantly beaded clothing and accessories. One accessory some people wear is a tight-fitting necklace called a choker. Chokers can be beaded from top to bottom and from side to side. One way of putting the beads together is using a lane stitch.

## You will need:

- strip of heavy material to fit around neck
- small, multi-coloured beads
- thread
- sewing needle
- velcro

## Steps

1. Take the material and draw vertical rows, or lanes, for your beads to follow.
2. Place one piece of velcro on the outside end of the material. Place the other piece on the inside of the other end.
3. Thread the needle, and knot one end of the thread.
4. Pass the needle through the material to secure the knot.
5. Put 5 to 10 beads onto the thread, and lay them in one of the lanes.
6. Take a small stitch at the end of the row, with the thread going down into the material and coming up where the next group of beads is to be placed.
7. Thread 5 to 10 more beads, and lay these beside to the previous row.
8. Stitch as before, and repeat.
9. When you have beaded the entire strip of material, put a few reinforcing stitches into the material. Then, cut the thread.
10. Your choker is now ready to wear. Put the choker around your neck, and fasten it with the velcro.

# Further Reading

Traditional Ktunaxa tales are told in *Ktunaxa Legends* by The Kootenai Culture Committee (University of Washington Press, 1997).

The Kootenai Culture Committee continues its storytelling in *Owl's Eyes and Seeking a Spirit* (2000).

# Websites

For information on the Ktunaxa people and their traditions, visit: **www.ktunaxa.org/who/index.html**.

To learn more about Ktunaxa clothing, homes, and tools, go to: **www.ktunaxamemories.ca**.

To see examples of Ktunaxa petroglyphs, visit: **http://files.fortsteele.ca/ history/maps/index.asp**.

# GLOSSARY

**Aboriginal:** original inhabitants of a country

**ancestors:** relatives who lived a very long time ago

**archaeologists:** scientists who study objects from the past to learn about people who lived long ago

**artifacts:** items, such as tools, made by a human being

**Christian:** a person who practises a religion based on the teachings of Jesus Christ

**culture:** the arts, beliefs, habits, and institutions characteristic of a community, people, or country

**docudrama:** a film or video that tells a fact-based story

**elders:** the older and more influential people of a community

**First Nations:** members of Canada's Aboriginal community who are not Inuit or Métis

**fur trade:** the exchange of furs for European goods

**gunwale:** the reinforced top edge of the side of a boat

**heritage:** the places, people, and culture of the past

**Interior Plains:** the rolling, low-lying land found in central Canada; sometimes called the Prairies

**migrating:** moving from one place to another

**moccasins:** soft leather shoes

**pemmican:** a mixture of dried meat and berries that has been pounded into powder and mixed with fat

**regalia:** fine clothes

**reserve lands:** lands set apart by the federal government for a special purpose, especially for the use by an Aboriginal group

**residential school:** schools where Aboriginal children were sent to live and learn

**sacred:** worthy of religious worship

**spirituality:** sacred or religious

**sturgeon:** a sharklike, bony fish

**vandalism:** the willful destruction of property

**videography:** the making of videos

# INDEX